BOOK OF TA·

The Beginners Guide to the Basic Fundamentals of Tattoo and Successful Tattooing

DON EDWARDS

Copyright @2021

Table of Contents

CHAPTER ONE

THE TATTOO

Why Get a Tattoo?

The aphorism of any individual who is thinking about getting a tattoo ought to be, "Think before you ink."

The shocking tales about the individuals who got a tattoo without much forethought are known to a great many people. For instance, bride-to-be's have been left standing at the altar after tattooing their fiancées' names on their ring fingers in high hopes, among others.

More or less, the point at which you are inebriated, high, in love or on a holiday, are the most exceedingly awful occasions to get a tattoo. You are bound to pick a design that looks similarly as awful as you may be going to feel the following morning at the point when you are tanked or high. On the off chance that you choose to tattoo your sweetheart's name on your lower arm, ensure it's for eternity, else you could end up loathing your arm just as much you do your ex. Individuals on holidays are likewise defenceless against settling on hurried choices, frequently bringing home gifts on their skin that don't accommodate their typical way of life by any stretch of the imagination.

Before you get a tattoo, you ought to plunk down and truly question your own inspirations for needing to do as such. For example, "since it would make your mom cry" is certifiably not a valid justification to get a tattoo. Getting a tattoo additionally once in a while doesn't accomplish the expectation of "evolving society" nor is it precisely an outflow of defiance to power. "Doing it since every other person is doing it" is likewise not a strong avocation.

Before you get that tattoo inked on your lower leg, ensure it won't make you feel sick each time you take a gander at it a long time from now.

There are a ton of valid justifications to get a tattoo and numerous that are not very good.

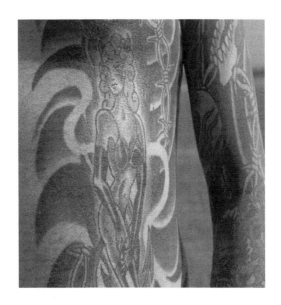

Valid Reasons to Get a Tattoo

The following constitutes good reasons to get a tattoo:

1. **Self-Expression**: Your unique sense of individuality can be conveyed to the world by means of tattoos, which are artistic creations. For example, a ghostly spirit tattooed on your arm will enable people identify you as one who is into the "undead scene." The tattoo can likewise give others some thought of your occupation.

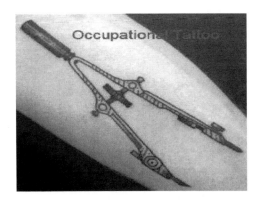

2. **Tribal Identity**: Marking a person as an individual of a clan or a gathering was the first aim of a tattoo. This sort of tattoo cautions others in the event that you end up having a place with some sort of gang (useful for them) and permits other close allies to distinguish you (useful for you).

3. **Spiritual Growth**: Numerous people will get a tattoo after they experience a revelation or act of faith that has prompted their survival against incredible chances. For instance, a cancer survivor who gets a tattoo, amongst others.

4. **For Spiritual Protection**: Taxi drivers will flaunt a tattoo St. Christopher on their arms to forestall mishaps out and about. An extremely recognizable tattoo for insurance is the eye inside the hand or the eye inside the triangle that

discovers its beginnings in the old Mediterranean. Crucifixes, consecrated hearts, St. Michael and divine beings or goddesses are regularly utilized for similar purposes.

5. **Marking Important Events**: Weddings, commemorations, divorces, enduring a conflict and different events in some cases warrant a tattoo. A few couples are getting tattoos set apart around the fourth finger of their left hand instead of settling on

the conventional wedding ring.

6. **Paying Homage**: At times a tattoo is in order after the demise of a big name, most loved pet or relative. Generally these tattoos are pictures appointed by a gifted craftsman who can duplicate similarities of such personages.

7. **To Enhance Luck**: Getting a tattoo to improve your luck is just about as old as crude man. Today, individuals who wish to court Lady Luck usually go for sets of dice, four leafed

clovers or Greek Goddess Fortuna marked on their arms.

8. **To Express Commitment**: Getting a tattoo in this day of "dispensable everything" is a declaration of obligation to yourself that it is until the end of time. The sages say that settling on an irreversible choice is useful for the spirit!

9. **Totem Symbols and Animals**: A few group believe a tattoo to be a declaration of their spirit or soul guide. Examples of this sort of tattoo are wolves,

pixies, angels, hummingbirds, tigers, butterflies, amongst others.

10. **As a Remembrance**: A few tattoos are utilized to recollect a cherished relative or pet that has died.

11. **Enhancing Sexuality**: There is a hypothesis that getting a tattoo on the lower back assists with opening up the base chakra (close to the lower part of the spine) and improves the kundalini (life power) that oversees such matters as endurance and sexuality. A

minuscule tattoo on the female hipbone or on the inward thigh is viewed as exceptionally sexy.

12. **Multiple Births**: In this period of fertility drugs, more moms than at any other time are bringing forth identical twins, triplets and quadruplets. Inking the lower part of the infants' feet is one approach to ensure that you can generally differentiate your kids from one another.

13. **To Make People Laugh**: Tattoos do have a method of "loosening things up"

with regards to beginning a discussion. There isn't anything amiss with adding a little levity to the world. After all humour breaks up all karma.

Awful Reasons to Get a Tattoo

1. To oppose authority. Individuals change the world and not tattoos.

2. To resemble a biker. This can genuinely blow up on you in the event that you run into a genuine biker who might be annoyed by your allocation of their ancestral markings.

3. "Everyone else is doing it!" is not a good reason to get a tattoo. Follow your gut sense, not the counsel of your companions.

4. To make your mom cry. This is definitely a lousy reason to get a tattoo.

CHAPTER TWO

TATTOOS' HISTORY

Primitive Tattoos

Skin was the principal material (or canvas) for workmanship (or art). Sticks and other sharp articles were the principal paintbrushes. Tattooing was the initial type of scarification. This entailed injuring oneself and pressing earth (dirt) or ashes into the scratch or cut to stain it forever. It is accepted that ancient man cut openings in his skin, burned sticks in the fire, let them cool and afterward applied the dark substance to the injury to make ancestral markings.

As tattooing included agony, blood and fire, crude man accepted the cycle delivered hallowed life powers. The letting of blood was likewise connected with a penance to the Gods. The image or creature type of the tattoo was thought to bring one protection from assault from that exact same creature.

Tattoos were likewise used to bring one's soul in alignment with the purpose of God, boost virility and fruitfulness, guarantee the safeguarding of the body after death and portray progressive systems and roles inside clans.

As skin doesn't protect that well there is little archeological proof that ancient individuals engaged in tattooing, albeit a couple of Paleolithic relics that have been found imply that the craft of tattooing is pretty much as old as humankind.

Art of the Funereal

Tattooing was a funereal art form in ancient history. Tattooing is depicted on Egyptian female figures dating from 4000 to 2000 years BC. Libyan figures from Seti's tomb (1330 B.C.) likewise feature tattooed arms and legs.

Primitive people, both ancient and modern, believed that the spirit or astral body resembled an invisible human body. This is consistent with a large number of contemporary occultist views regarding the astral body. Tattoos are used to ensure that the spirit is able to enter the spirit world without being disturbed by demonic entities. The indigenous peoples of Borneo believe that the appropriate tattoo ensures a speedy transition to the other side and a guaranteed favorable vocation in the spirit realm.

According to legend, the ancient Egyptians popularized tattooing throughout the world. Egypt's third and fourth dynasties built pyramids and established worldwide nations that governed Crete, Greece, Persia, and Arabia. By 2000 B.C., the art of tattooing had spread to Southeast Asia, where it was adopted by the Ainu (western Asian nomads) during their migrations to Japan. In other parts of the world, the Shans of China taught the craft to the Burmese, who continue to incorporate tattooing into their religious ceremonies.

Today, tattoos are still utilized to establish a spiritual link with deceased family members and loved ones. Although these tattoos are more uncommon, they frequently take the form of hearts with initials, tombstones with parent's initials, or heavenly symbols such as five, six, or seven pointed stars.

Branding

Simultaneously, the Japanese developed an interest in the art, but solely for its decorative qualities. The Horis — the ancient Japanese tattoo artists — were indisputable masters of color tattooing. Their innovative use of colours, perspective, and unique designs transformed the practice. Japan inherited Chinese culture during the first millennium A.D. and restricted tattooing to branding criminals.

The Thracians used the craft differently in the Balkans. According to Herodotus (500 B.C.), aristocrats were tattooed to demonstrate their social rank to the world.

Although early Europeans dabbled in tattooing, it was not until they encountered new tribes in the South Pacific that they properly revived the art form. Tattoos were brought to modern Europe through acquaintance with the tattoos of Polynesian and American Indian tribes. Indeed, the term originates from the Tahitian verb *tattau*, which meaning "to mark."

The majority of tattoos' early applications were decorative. However, a lot of civilizations used this technique for utilitarian purposes. The Goths, a Germanic barbarian tribe infamous for pillaging Roman cities, brand their slaves with tattoos. Additionally, the Romans tattooed slaves and criminals.

In the middle of the third century, tattooing became connected with criminality in the Mediterranean region. The crime, the penalty, and the names of the criminal's victims would all be branded on their foreheads.

Slaves with tattoos were never allowed to become citizens in ancient Greece and Rome, even if they were able to purchase their freedom. This was because tattoos were seen to be demeaning to the bearer. In essence, the tattoos served as permanent reminders of wrongdoing. Eventually, people who were tattooed as a form of punishment developed an appreciation for their markings. Today, tattoos remain a badge of prestige for criminals.

Tattoos were a rite of passage in Tahiti and served as a record of a person's life. When men reached adulthood and married, they were marked. When the Turkish Ottoman Empire ruled Bosnia and Herzegovina, military authorities tattooed all troops to identify them in case they evaded conscription.

Clan Insignia

Additionally, primitive peoples employed tattoos to create what are known as clan markings.

These markings proved useful during battle for distinguishing foe from ally. Additionally, these tattoos ensured that you would be reunited with your friends in heaven following your death.

Family and marriage tattoos were also clan insignia that permitted bereaved spouses to reunite in the afterlife. A classic example of this is the ancient Ainu tribe, who believed that a bride without a tattoo would be transported directly to Gehenna, their version of hell.

In the Americas, indigenous people tattooed their bodies or faces with simple pricking. In

California, some indigenous cultures colored the scratches. Certain northern cultures living in and around the Arctic Circle (primarily Inuit) punctured the skin with a needle and threaded a soot-coated thread through it. The South Pacific community used a little rake-like device to tap pigment into the punctured skin.

In New Zealand, the Maori used the body as though it were a piece of wood while creating their world-famous *moko* tattoos. They would carve intricate shallow grooves on the face and buttocks with a little bone-cutting tool and color them.

They were able to improve the efficiency of the technology by trading with Europeans and employing metal tools instead of bone tools.

A "moko," which translates as "to strike or tap," is a long-standing Maori tattooing technique. This art form has existed for over a thousand years and has been unaffected by time and colonization. It served as a means of identification for rank, genealogy, tribal history, marriage eligibility, beauty, and virility.

Moko designs were carved into the skin with care. Traditionally, Maori women were only permitted to have tattoos around their lips, around the chin, and occasionally on their nostrils. A woman with big blue lips was regarded as extremely attractive.

Passage Rituals

Adolescents were also tattooed by primitive people as a rite of passage. The belief was that if a young boy was unable to endure the pain of a tattoo at such a young age, he would be rendered ineffective in war. Similarly, if a young girl is unable of coping with the agony of a tattoo, she will be incapable of coping with the anguish of childbirth. Many of these children eventually received a tattoo designating them as an outsider of the tribe.

Additionally, totem animals are a popular motif in prehistoric tattoos. Totem animals like as snakes, frogs, butterflies, wolves, or bears indicated that the individual had absorbed the animal's physical power. In certain cultures, the totem animal is believed to have a spiritual connection with the tattoo wearer and works as a spirit guide.

From the South Pacific to South America, primitive cultures have tattooing ceremonies that are governed by customs. Typically, the tattooed individual is segregated from others, smeared, isolated from the opposite sex, or fed a particular diet.

From prehistoric times to the present, Hawaiians have venerated unique tattoo gods. The designs connected with each God are kept locked away in temples, and tattooing is performed by priests.

Each tattoo session begins with a prayer to the tattoo gods, pleading for the surgery to go smoothly and for the final designs to be beautiful.

Charms of Love

Tattoos were often employed as love charms in the ancient and primordial societies. Frequently, the dye for these tattoos is produced from supernatural materials. For example, the dye for an ancient Burmese love charm is prepared using a deep purple pigment called vermilion along with the skins of a trout and a spotted lizard. Typically, this tattoo was a little triangle formed by three dots that was disguised by clothing to prevent people from identifying it.

Celtic knots, hearts, cherubs, the Venus symbol, and love

goddesses are modern-day analogues of magic love tattoos.

Physical Fitness

Tattoos were frequently done in ancient Asian societies to maintain long-term bodily health. Tibetans associated shapes known as mantra wheels with lengthy periods of chanting. These motifs were tattooed on chakra (energy points) on the body to aid the tattooee in achieving physical, emotional, and spiritual balance. Occasionally, medicinal colors were used to produce tattoos and were applied to acupuncture locations on the body in an attempt to cure chronic health problems and diseases.

Numerous cultures allow for the tattooing of an image of a God or Goddess on an acupuncture point or an affected portion of the body in an attempt to heal it. Hanuman, the Monkey God, was tattooed on dislocated shoulders in India. Maori women in their later years tattooed their lips and faces to protect their vision from deterioration. Ainu women tattooed a Goddess on their flesh in order to confuse the bad spirits that gave disease with the Goddess and run in fear.

Peonies are believed to bring love into the life of a young woman in China.

Best Wishes

Throughout history, tattoos have been believed to bring the wearer good fortune. In China, it is believed that tattooing one's animal astrological sign, such as The Pig or The Horse, brings good fortune. Koi, carp, or goldfish images were believed to bring the bearer fortune and wealth.

In Burma, a tattoo of a parrot on the shoulder is believed to bring good fortune. In Thailand, a scroll depicting Buddha in a meditation pose is said to attract Lady Luck. American soldiers in Vietnam wore card tattoos such as the Ace of Spades and the Ten of Diamonds to ward off bad luck and venereal disease.

Celtic Ink

In the 1970s, America's counter culture rediscovered the splendor of primordial and tribal taboos. The most imitated designs originate mostly in Borneo, Japan, and the South Pacific islands. Celtic tattoos became extremely popular in the 1980's, owing to the popularity of Wiccan and pagan religions among young people.

The majority of contemporary Celtic designs are inspired by historical scrolls known as the Irish Illuminated Manuscripts, which were made between the sixth and seventh centuries. Due to the Celts' lack of written history, designs can also be found in old stone and metalwork. Prior to the sixth century, these ancient peoples frequently tattooed or painted their faces and bodies to ward off evil spirits and assure military victory.

From Britain and Ireland to Scotland, the knotwork tattooing tradition inherited from Celtic literature expanded. Viking conquerors subsequently adopted many Celtic motifs into their own culture, frequently interlacing totem animals into the designs.

Celtic knots are "zoomorphic," which means that each of the

design's strands connects to or spirals into another. Frequently, these designs will end graphically with representations of animals' paws, heads, and tails, as well as other natural symbols. These animals served as mascots for several Celtic tribes and ethnicities.

Additionally, Roman documents show that ancient British and Scottish peoples may have been tattooed prior to combat. Ancient Gaulish stones also depict leaders with tattooed faces. Woad, a plant that generates blue dye, was used to create these tattoos. A Pict skeleton discovered frozen in Siberia's permafrost indicates that these pre-Celtic peoples tattooed utilizing puncture marks to create animal forms and outlines using woad as the color.

The Romans frequently entrusted their children to Celtic teachers. Numerous instructors were Druidic priests.

Aetius, a long-dead Roman physician, provided an ancient Roman recipe for tattoo ink:

- ✓ 1 pound bark of Egyptian pine wood
- ✓ 2 oz. tarnished bronze powdered with vinegar
- ✓ 2 oz. gall (insect egg deposits)

- ✓ 1 ounce vitriol (iron sulphate)

Combine thoroughly and sift. Soak powder in a solution of two parts water to one part leek juice. Leek juice should be used to cleanse the skin that will be tattooed. Using needles, prick the design until blood is drawn. Ink should be rubbed in.

Children, do not attempt this at home!

Tattoos of Pilgrims

Tattooing was prohibited in Europe and the Middle East due to the growth of Christian and Islamic religions. The book of Leviticus in the Bible's Old

Testament states, "Ye shalt not make any cuts in your flesh for the dead, nor shall you stamp any marks upon you: I am the Lord." This anti-tattooing sentiment resulted in the practice disappearing for almost two thousand years, as both Christians and Moslems venerate the Old Testament.

Despite the broad acceptance of this religious concept, pilgrims in the Middle Ages continued to have tattoos upon reaching the Holy Land to demonstrate to family and friends that they had made the trek. Coptic priests sat outside Jerusalem's walls, waiting for travellers, and practiced this type of tattooing. Typically, these tattoos consisted of a simple cross, but other pilgrims chose more ornate symbols commemorating their journey, such as the Pieta or St. George defeating the Dragon.

Moslem pilgrims who travelled to Mecca and Medina also returned with remembrance tattoos. These Moslem pilgrims believed that by being cremated at death, they would be purified by fire and therefore forgiven for violating Levictus' decree.

Asian Tattoos

In Japan, tattooing peaked in the 18th century, with designs based on traditional watercolor paintings, woodcuts, and picture books.

Japanese tattoo artists were frequently also ukiyoe woodblock artists, who simply substituted long, pointed needles for their wood carving blades. This lengthy procedure culminated in the creation of the uniquely Japanese traditional tattoo art form known as horimono.

Tattoos on Sailors and Military Personnel

When European explorers first arrived in the New World, they learned that tattooing was a significant element of Native Americans' stone-age culture. Geometric designs and dots were popular across the majority of tribes and were used to commemorate an individual's entry into puberty. Numerous tribes, like the Sioux Indians, believed that a tattoo was required to enter the other world.

After over two thousand years away from popular culture, the tattoo phenomenon resurfaced when explorers brought accounts of it home after seeing specimens in North and South America.

From the 1600's to the 1940's, sailors tattooed a chicken on one foot and a pig on the other to protect themselves from drowning. During WWII, the large emblem that guarded sailors against drowning were twin propellers (one on each buttock) intended to drive you to the shore symbolically.

Bluebird images inked on the chest were frequently used to indicate how many kilometres a sailor had travelled at sea. Each bluebird represented 5,000 nautical kilometres. If a sailor travelled south of the equator, he might have a tattoo of Neptune on his leg. If a sailor passed the international dateline, he acquired the right to wear a dragon tattoo. A tattoo of a hula girl indicated that the sailor had visited Honolulu. The sailor's body was tattooed with female lingerie and stockings, indicating that he had been on more than one trip.

In the pre-civil war era of the United States, Chatham Square in New York City became the epicenter of tattooing. Sailors, gang members, and low-lifes frequented this region known for its beer halls and prostitution parlors.

Sailors spent their long hours at sea "pricking" drawings into their own or their companions' flesh. These designs included elements of patriotism and protection. Often, gunpowder was added to the ink, as gunpowder was believed to have mystical longevity and protection properties. Due to their considerable travel, mariners of the era were familiar with tattoos. They had seen the dragons of China, the Christian charms and evil eyes of the populace, and the intricate decorations worn by the folks of Edo and Yokohama. Sailors dressed in these exotic designs travelled through the port of New York on a daily basis, significantly impacting and enlarging the concept of "tattoo."

Thousands of soldiers from New York were conscripted into the Union Army with the commencement of the Civil War. During the conflict, the desire for patriotic tattoos increased dramatically, and thousands of individuals were tattooed on the battlefield. Popular designs frequently featured images of significant wars complete with sky and terrain.

Automated Tattoo Machines

During the final decade of the nineteenth century, Samuel O'Reilly's creation of the electric tattoo machine revolutionized tattooing. The time necessary to execute a design decreased from hours to minutes, relegating the art form to stock designs that were displayed like art on the walls of the tattoo parlor. Additionally, much of this tattooing occurred in the back rooms of beer halls and barbershops.

In the years to come, O'Reilly's machine would undergo significant upgrades, as would the formation of tattoo equipment manufacturing companies. This equipment served as a prototype for the tattoo gun that is now the industry standard.

In the 1920's and 1930's, tattoo styles modified to incorporate comic strip characters such as Mickey Mouse and Felix the Cat, Lindbergh's crossing, silver screen stars and starlets, and words popularized in the press.

Cosmetic tattooing began during this time period as well. Numerous artists cater to both male and female consumers, offering services such as moles and beauty marks, rosy cheeks, permanent eyeliner, and red lips.

Contemporary Tattoos

Tattooing for the sake of art became popular in the 1960s, and nowadays it is typical to see someone with a tattoo on their shoulder, hip, or ankle. Celtic tattoos, as well as primitive tattoos, have had a renaissance in recent years.

Certain individuals collect tattoos in the same way they collect antiques or pieces of art. Others are drawn to ultra-slim designs that are a product of twenty-first-century thought, such as biomechanical designs (which resemble muscles beneath the skin) and designs that imitate the inside workings of cyborgs.

In the 1970s, artists trained in traditional fine art disciplines embraced tattooing and introduced the business to creative imagery and drawing techniques.

They gained new color palettes, fineness of detail, and aesthetic potential as a result of advancements in electric needle guns and paints. Numerous local tattoo shops have also changed physically as an increasing number of operators adopted equipment and methods similar to those found in medical clinics – notably in locations where tattooing is governed by government health standards.

Tattooing's cultural position has steadily developed over the years, from an anti-social pastime in the 1940s to a contemporary fashion statement in the 2000s. Tattooing was first popularized and promoted by famous rock bands such as the Rolling Stones in the early 1970s, by the late 1980s, had gained acceptance in mainstream society. Today, tattoos are frequently seen on rock stars, professional athletes, ice skating champions, fashion models, and movie stars, as well as other public people who influence the direction of current culture.

Two unique tattoo business classes have arisen during the last fifteen years. The first is the "tattoo parlor," which extols an urban criminal culture, advertises itself with flashy external signs, and operates in less than sanitary conditions. The second type is the "tattoo art studio," which frequently offers unique and fine art designs, all of the amenities of a high-end beauty salon, and only by appointment. The fine art tattoo studio of today attracts the same type of clientele as a jewelry store, fashion boutique, or high-end antique shop.

Today, tattooing is the sixth fastest growing retail industry in the United States. Middle-class suburban women are the fastest rising demographic group seeking tattoo services.

Government agencies acknowledge tattooing as both an art form and a vocation. Due to the fact that tattoo-related artwork is considered great art, tattoo designs are frequently shown in museum and gallery exhibitions throughout the United States, Canada, and Europe.

Nowadays, almost any picture is fair game for a tattoo, from Andy Warhol images to Teletubbies to instant messaging happy face emblems. Your tattoo design options are only limited by your imagination!

CHAPTER THREE

TATTOOS' STYLES

Tattoos - Stock and Custom

Tattoo designs are classified into two categories: stock (sometimes referred to as flash) tattoos and personalized (or custom) tattoos.

Stock or flash tattoos are the images that adorn tattoo parlor walls.

Typically, these images include perennial favorites like anchors, hearts, skulls, dragons, butterflies, and crucifixes. These are the designs that the tattoo artist is willing to create on a fixed cost basis.

Generally, custom tattoos are more expensive. In this situation, you contract the artist to create the image you desire by bringing in an image or mix of images to be recreated on your flesh.

Greater is Always Better

While any image can be tattooed onto your body, some may appear better on paper than on your skin. By and large, a large, bold, straightforward image is more illuminating than a small, detailed image. Larger photos have simply more impact.

American tattooist Walt Dailey summarizes the "larger is better" debate by stating, "When a gorgeous, large, powerful bear head design gets shrunk down, it resembles an angry hamster's face."

When it comes to tattoos, the maxim "larger is better" applies. If you find yourself staring at a collection of intricate patterns filled with curlicues, landscapes, and portraits, you may want to consider the KISS motto adopted by American astronauts: "KEEP IT SIMPLE STUPID." Bear in mind that you may always embellish your tattoo later if you are dissatisfied with a simple design.

Tattoo Science

By modern standards, early tattooing techniques appear pretty barbarous. South American cultures covered the skin with pigment or dirt after scratching or pricking it. The Inuit pierced the skin and inserted a soot-covered needle into open wounds.

The Maoris pierced the skin with a bone-cutting tool and then covered the cuts with ash and other colours. Today, traditional

Japanese tattoos are still created by manually puncturing the skin and dabbing colour into the wounds.

Fortunately, because to O'Reilly's electrically driven tattoo machine, tattooing techniques have advanced significantly.

The Tattoo Machine

Because the base of this modern tattooing machine resembles the handle of a pistol, it is occasionally referred to as a tattoo gun. The tattoo machine is composed of three components: a gun-shaped base, an enclosed motor, and a tube containing the ink and needles.

The machine pulsates vertically, puncturing the first two layers of skin with needles. The impact of the needle striking the skin forces the ink from the tube through the epidermis.

By varying the number of needles in the machine, the varied lines required to build up the tattoo can be created. A set of needles arranged in a circular arrangement creates solid lines. Typically, shading needles are aligned vertically or horizontally in slots.

Ink for Tattoos

Tattoo ink is not, in fact, ink. It is a suspension of pigments in a carrier solution. Unfortunately, there is no way to tell exactly what is contained in tattoo ink, as producers are not obligated to disclose the ingredients. Additionally, the formulae for specific colored inks are as well guarded as the Kentucky Fried Chicken recipe.

The majority of tattoo inks are known to be composed of metal salts, while some may contain vegetable-based colours. Given that the majority of tattoo inks contain components that are unknown even to the tattooist, it's difficult to forecast if you'll have an allergic reaction to the ink. Although allergic reactions are uncommon, they are something to consider if you have particularly sensitive skin. The most typical symptom is an itchy, raised appearance of the skin, which can take up to a week to manifest.

Fundamental Inking Styles

As with any other medium of expression, tattoos might take the form of line drawings, paintings, cartoons, caricatures, or even airbrushed works. Tattoos, like paintings, can be divided into numerous genres such as impressionism, realism, cubism, and so on. Each style combines distinct aesthetic components that a large number of people are unfamiliar with. Thus, here is a look at tattoos as an art form, not as a symbol of rebellion, a health threat, or a display of "coolness."

The following is a brief overview of several popular tattoo styles.

1. **Work in black and gray**: This style developed in America's jail system, where colored ink was scarce. These tattoos have the same warmth and depth as a charcoal drawing.

2. **Traditional**: This tattoo style is characterized by aggressive black outlines and pitch black shading juxtaposed with extremely brilliant colors. The style is said to have originated in the 1930s and 1940s on military stations.

3. **Fineline**: These delicate tattoos are extremely intricate and are frequently used in conjunction with black and gray art. Additionally, fineline is frequently employed to convey a realistic picture of an image. Fineline images cannot be overly intricate, as the image may degrade

into a splotch or a shadow over time.

4.   **Tribal**:   These   are silhouettes   in   black.   The majority   are   inspired   by ancient   tribal   motifs.   A frequent   modern   variation on   this   style   is   to   alter   a classic   design   to   give   it   a tribal   appearance.

Numerous current styles are derived from ancient South Pacific Island styles. Spikes, swirls, and spines are common design components in these tattoos, which are usually artistic, creative depictions. Tribal tattoos are frequently created to complement or enhance a particular region of the body. For instance, a tribal tattoo may snake down the lower back's curves.

5. **Realistic**: Typically, they are portraits or landscapes that replicate the precise detail of a photograph. They are often done in black and white because emulating images in colors requires an expert tattoo artist. Occasionally, this style is

referred to as photo-realism.

6. **Oriental**: Typically, the oriental form of tattooing uses the entire body as a canvas rather than just a few images here and there. On a full arm or across the entire back, images are employed to build a story or myth. Typically, this is quite fantastical and audacious, yet color work that is meticulous. The most typical oriental tattoos are large murals of dragons, flowers, fish, and other creatures. A dominating

picture, such as a dragon, may be surrounded by beautiful, fluid-like swirls of color. Oriental tattoos frequently adhere to the norms of Japanese perspective, a style of art concerned with symmetry and balance. Additionally, the symbols used in Japanese tattoos frequently have deeper meanings. For instance, a carp tattoo symbolizes money and prosperity.

7. **Celtic**: These tattoos in the silhouette style have broad, dramatic black lines and a

sharp angle. A Viking derivation of the Celtic style, the Viking style incorporates mythological creatures such as griffins. They are typically completed entirely in black ink. Celtic tattoos, due to their difficulty, are frequently best made by an artist who specializes in the style.

8. **Biomechanical**:

Oftentimes, these tattoos
feature   machinery
intermingled   with   human
flesh.   A   common
biomechanical tattoo design
may feature a human hand,
arm, or chest entangled in
machinery components such
as   screws,   wheels,   or

pulleys. As a result, an image of a creature that appears to be half-robot, half-human is created. This style of tattoo is influenced by films like "Alien."

9.   **Cartoons and caricatures**: These tattoos are characterized by their

bold lines and frequently
hilarious allusions to
traditional (or classic)
tattoos.

CHAPTER FOUR

MOTIFS AND SYMBOLISM IN TATTOOS

There are simply as many tattoo motifs and symbols as there are artistic ideas in the world. When selecting a design, it may be beneficial to consider the following:

- ✓ What motivates me?
- ✓ What am I striving for?
- ✓ What provides me with strength?

These three straightforward questions should spark your gray matter into thinking about what constitutes meaningful "marking" for you.

The following is a list of some of the most popular tattoo motifs and symbols.

Animals

Animals are frequently selected as tattoo subjects for a variety of reasons. It could simply be that you enjoy the four-legged furry creature. Perhaps you're doing it to honor the memory of a departed pet.

Often, though, the animal is chosen because the individual identifies with the creature's strengths and attributes and seeks to emphasize these characteristics in his or her own character, or because the animal serves as a shamanic spirit guide for them.

The following is a discussion of some of the characteristics of animals that are frequently depicted in tattoo art.

1. Apes and Monkeys are Chinese Astrological Signs that symbolize contentment, freedom from persecution, and sex (in the South Pacific).

2. Bats - a sign of immortality and happiness, psychic abilities, and vampires (Pagan).

3. Bears - a symbol of strength, protection, fortitude, and rebirth (Native American).

4.   Bees - messengers of God (Greek), soul bearers to paradise (Native American), and bringers of wealth (Ukrainian and Viking).

5.   Bison and Buffalo - instils a sense of contemplation (Native American).

6.   Boars - a symbol of victory and prosperity (Roman).

7.   Bulls — strength, motivation, and dominance (Native American), Taurus's astrological emblem.

8.   Cats are divine; they have a connection to Egyptian and alien spirits and provide

psychic protection (Wiccan, Pagan).

9.   Cows - a holy mother goddess emblem in India. A red cow represents hope (India, China).

10. Crickets - a symbol of reincarnation, creativity, and good fortune (Pagan).

11. Deer - epilepsy treatment, visions, dreams, associated with the Greek Goddess of the Hunt Diana, beauty (Native American)

12. Dogs symbolize loyalty, service, trust, affection, and a carefree (or easy) existence.

13. Donkey - fertility, health, happiness, and good fortune (Asian).

14. Fox - shapeshifter, cleverness, and magical abilities (Pagan, Wiccan).

15. Frog – mediumship (Native American), delivering prosperity (Chinese).

16. Gazelle - emblem of health (Africa).

17. Goats - symbol of Pan (Greek, Celtic, and Wiccan), Western Astrological sign of Capricorn, Chinese Astrological sign.

18. Hares - Celtic god Brigid's symbol, moon symbol (Wiccan).

19. Horses - American astrological sign of liberty and strength; Chinese astrological sign.

20. Jaguars are associated with shamanism (African, Nordic).

21. Lamb - Christian emblem; Ram - Western astrological sign of Aries.

22. Lions - a sign of the sun (Roman, Greek), of protection (Africa), and of mercy and gentleness (lion cubs) (Native American).

23. Ox - prosperity, employment Chinese zodiac sign.

24. Pigs - Prosperity and happiness (Chinese), rebirth (Celtic), motorbike or chopper owner (Biker).

25. Rabbit - Luck (Celtic), manifestation abilities (Pagan).

26. Rat - Imagination, cleverness, Chinese zodiac sign.

27. Rooster - Celtic sexual fertility symbol; Chinese astrological sign.

28. Scorpion - the soul's fire, sensuality (Egyptian), Western astrological emblem for Scorpio, Chinese astrological sign.

29. Tiger - virility, strength (Celtic); Chinese astrological sign.

30. Tortoises & Turtles - wisdom (Celtic), wealth (Chinese).

Biker

Purists might argue that a tattoo does not qualify as a legitimate biker tattoo if it does not include the Harley Davidson insignia. Although the Harley Davidson insignia are virtually identical, many are embellished with other symbols such as jaguars, eagles, feathers, skulls, dragons, bats, flames, and hot babes.

Many bikers choose to have a tattoo of their custom chopper on their arm. Those who enjoy customizing choppers frequently have tattoos of nuts and bolts, screws, wheel hubs, and other motorcycle components. The picture of a bike's wheel or the bike itself roaring in a cloud of flames is extremely popular.

Three dots anyplace on the body, as well as the usage of Old English Goth script, are prominent indicators of a biker tattoo.

Although firearms and anti-authoritarian statements are also frequent in biker tattoos, many of them are surprisingly placid and feature the standard flowers, poker hands, Mom tributes, and blazing skulls seen on non-biker body parts.

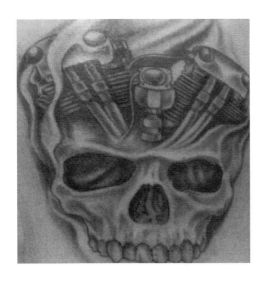

Biomechanical

Tattoos with a biomechanical theme frequently represent technology mixed with human flesh. H. R. Giger, who created the creature from the Alien films, is the father of all biomechanical designs. A typical biomechanical piece may portray a human hand, arm, or chest entangled in machinery like as screws, wheels, or pulleys. As a result, an image of a creature that appears to be half-robot, half-human is created.

Biomechanical tattoos are considered fetish tattoos and are inspired by Salvador Dali's paintings, fetishism, and Satanism.

Skeletons, Skulls, and Bones

Bone tattoos are as ancient as shamanism, healing, and magic. This is most likely derived from the ancient superstitious idea that donning death protects against death. The belief is that any evil that comes close to the bearer of such a tattoo will be scared away by the image of death on his or her body.

Skulls also symbolize esoteric lore and psychic abilities. Tattoos of skulls are quite common among bikers, Goths, Wiccans, and members of the military.

Birds

Birds are symbolic of the soul's freedom and the imagination's flight. Bird feather tattoos symbolize respect, victory, and shamanic abilities. Feathers from birds are still used for a variety of magical uses, including energy transmission and decoration of spiritual devices such as dreamcatchers. Bird tattoos are prevalent in virtually every culture.

The following is a brief, but by no means exhaustive, summary of the symbolism associated with birds, which frequently occur as tattoo themes:

1. Bluebird - a traditional "sailor" tattoo that symbolizes happiness, safe travels.

2. Crane - a Chinese symbol of health, fidelity, and marriage.

3. The crow is a Celtic and Roman death messenger, a

Native American Indian Spirit Guide, and a Chinese esoteric wisdom sign.

4. Cuckoo - a pagan symbol of weddings, second sight, and transformation.

5. Dove - a universal emblem of peace and love, a Christian religion's sign of Christ Consciousness.

6. Eagles - a biker and patriotic emblem, a Native American symbol of strength, a Greek and Roman symbol of a leader, an Egyptian and Celtic symbol of the "bearer of souls" beyond death.

7. Geese - a symbol of Canada, a symbol of fresh beginnings.

8. Hummingbirds - a love charm in Celtic and African Voodoo traditions.

9. Magpie - an American Southwest symbol for wealth and protection.

10. Owl - a universal symbol of wisdom and wisdom from the Gods.

11. Peacock - a universal symbol of immortality, dignity, and authority.

12. Ravens - a Celtic symbol for battle victory, a pagan

symbol for messages from the dead.

13. Robin - an enduring (or ancient) symbol of benevolence and fertility.

14. Sparrow - a Christian emblem of faith.

15. Storks - traditionally used to announce the birth of a child, a global symbol of fertility, a guardian of the old (North American Indians), and a symbol of justice (Greece).

16. Swans - a classic love sign, a messenger of the Greek God of communication

Apollo, and a lunar emblem (Celtic and Pagan).

17. Wren - a protective charm against drowning (Sailor), as well as possessing magical or occult qualities (Wiccan and Pagan).

Butterflies, Insects, and Bugs

Butterfly and dragonfly tattoos are on the lighter side of the "bug" theme.

Butterflies are renowned as a symbol of inspiration, liberation, and metamorphosis. In almost every culture, the three stages of the butterfly's existence signify the three stages of life (birth, death, and rebirth). The Monarch butterfly represents safe trips in Native American Indian traditions, owing to the insect's capacity to fly hundreds of kilometers during its yearly migration season. Butterflies are believed to transport the spirits of the deceased to heaven in several pagan and Celtic cultures.

Women adore butterflies.

Dragonflies are truly magical creatures, and their gleaming bodies and glowing wings make for an excellent unisex tattoo. Dragonflies are considered to be a symbol of harmony, good fortune, and ancient knowledge. Additionally, they are believed to bring prophetic dreams and to protect against nightmares.

Spiders are on the darker side of things. Spiders are a prominent emblem for Goths, bikers, pagans, and punks. In Greek mythology, the spider was identified with Ariadne, the Greek Goddess of enchantment and mythology.

Characters from Cartoons and Animated Films

Stock cartoon graphics licensed specifically for tattooing are currently a large business in North America. On the Internet, one can now acquire photos of Betty Boop, Scooby Doo, Mickey Mouse, Batman, Spider-Man, Superman, the Tasmanian Devil, Babar the Elephant, and Nemo, among a plethora of other animated characters.

Anime action figures, which the majority of us are familiar with from manga cartoons, are also a large business in the tattoo industry, including iconic characters such as Hello Kitty, Emily, and Sailor Moon.

Of course, a large number of people have circumvented the licensing process and obtained their own customized copies of these cartoon characters. Cartoon figures in sinful poses are also a popular motif in tattooing, and are frequently utilized to convey one's vices creatively.

Caricatures and cartoons have always been an intrinsic part of tattooing, dating all the way back to the 1920s, when sailors visiting New York were entertained by drawings of Betty Boop and the stick-figure Mickey Mouse.

Generally, though, any portrait or figure can be turned into a cartoon.

Celts and Irish

Celtic tattoos are primarily defined by their interlacing knots, which are continuous loops with no beginning or finish. Occasionally, the theme incorporates animals or a zoomorphic design styled into a spiral.

Even though the symbolism of many of the images has been lost to time, knotwork motifs are iconic of the Celtic countries. Celtic tattoos are characterized by trees, cauldrons, shamrocks, spirals, horned gods, wheels, mandalas, serpents, druids, and gloomy jewels.

The interlacing of the knots represents the repeated crossover of the physical and spiritual realms. The never-ending course of the strands could symbolize the enduring nature of life, love, and faith.

Tattoos on Celebrities

What better way to pay tribute to a superstar than to incorporate him or her into your skin? This can be accomplished by portraiture, as in the classic black-and-white portraits of Elvis Presley or John F. Kennedy, or by emulating the tattoo of another renowned figure.

Since the 1960s, tattoos have been an integral part of the personae of the wealthy and famous, and it appears as though everyone from Gillian Anderson to Ben Affleck has one. Even the generally placid Barbie Doll was offered in the early 1970s with a huge flower tattoo beneath her ribs.

The AC/DC band emblem, the Rolling Stones' red lips and tongue insignia, and the KISS band logo are all notable tattoos. Portraits of Kiss's Gene Simmons, Brian Jones (previously of the Rolling Stones), Marilyn Monroe, John Lennon, Frank Sinatra ("I got you under my skin"), and Jim Morrison have been among his favorites. Kurt Cobain is also a recent favorite of the "Teen Spirit" set.

Another option is to replicate a celebrity's tattoo.

Celebrity tattoos have become the stuff of tabloid legend. Angelina Jolie, who has seven tattoos on her body, recently had a tiger etched into her skin in Tibet, yet many question if she would ever get rid of her large black Billy Bob tattoo on her forearm. Drew Barrymore, Courtney Love, and Cher are three additional female celebrities that are well-known for their penchant for ink.

Johnny Depp made headlines ten years ago when he changed the name of his tattoo from Winona Forever to Wino Forever. Pamela Anderson is well-known for her barb-wired forearm and for renaming a tattoo on her left ring finger "Tommy" (a tribute to her ex-husband Tommy Lee) to "Mommy."

Celestial Planets, Stars, and Suns

Planets, stars, and their associated symbols are extremely popular tattoo motifs. Perhaps one of the most prominent planetary glyphs and symbols is the interconnected symbol for Mars and Venus. This symbol represents the perpetual dance of male and female energies.

From early youth, the sun has been a symbol of glory, accomplishment, money, love, and prosperity. The moon is an occult symbol that represents the subconscious, intuition, sexual and esoteric mysteries, and the supernatural forces. Mercury is a planet that represents the Roman God of communication and the creative arts. Venus is the planet of love, Mars is the planet of war, and Saturn is the planet of discipline and acceptance of one's lot in life.

Each planet in the solar system likewise has its own Western Zodiac sign equivalent. For example, those born under the signs of Libra or Taurus should wear a Venus glyph or picture of the planet. The glyphs for the astrological symbols also make excellent tattoos, particularly if you're sick of people asking you "what's your sign?" as a pick up line.

Stars are frequently found as esoteric symbols, and the significance of each given star symbol is determined by its point count. The pentagram with five points is a potent emblem of protection and balance. It is symbolic of the human form and is associated with pagan and Wiccan beliefs.

The six-pointed hexagram is a potent symbol of God's contact with mortals, of God's interaction with humanity. It is associated with Kabbalah and is frequently referred to as the Star of David.

Due to its association with the number seven, the septagram or seven-pointed star is a sign of integration and the mystical. It is associated with classical astrology's seven planets, as well as other seven-fold systems such as the Hindu chakras.

The eight-pointed star, or octagram, symbolizes completion and rejuvenation. The I Ching's trigrams, the pagan wheel of the year, and ancient Egypt's Ogdoad are all eight-fold systems.

The nonagram or nine-pointed star is a symbol of accomplishment and stability, however it is a fluid stability. Additionally, it is associated with nine-fold systems, like the nine Taoist kanji.

Commemorative

Commemorative tattoos are worn to commemorate or mark a

significant event, such as a death, a global calamity, or a military victory. The majority of commemorative tattoos are "custom tattoos" that incorporate a variety of features to create a really unique object.

Commemorative tattoos can also be used to commemorate the loss of a loved one, a birth, or the enduring nature of a unique relationship.

Tattoos on Criminals and Prisoners

The symbolism of prison and criminal tattoos is a source of genuine esoteric fascination for some and a source of genuine concern for the police. A tattoo can reveal three things about a prisoner: "who he is, where he has been, and what he has done."

As these types of tattoos are frequently performed in prison, they are usually done freehand with ink from a pen. Sewing needles are used to create images and words. Additionally, prisoners create their own tattoo machines using a ball point pen, a guitar string, and a nine volt battery.

Police frequently use tattoo imagery to identify parolees and criminals. For instance, a downward-facing gun indicates that the man loves to be armed. Images of walls, towers, and barbwire indicate that he has been imprisoned for an extended period of time.

The following is a list of the symbolism linked with traditional prison tattoos:

1.   Clock faces without hands = Serving Time.

2.   Spiders or cobwebs on shoulders = Serving Time.

3.   Tombstones with numbers on them = Number of years spent in jail.

4.   Tombstones with R.I.P. and numbers on them =

Mourning the death of a buddy who died on the inside.

5.   Eight balls = Indicates being "out of sync" or having terrible luck.

6.   One smiling smile and one sobbing face equals gang member, "play now, pay later."

7.   SWP is an anagram for Supreme White Power.

8.   The term "Peckerwood" refers to Male White Pride.

9.   Featherwood refers to Female White Pride.

10. "100% Pure" refers to a white pride tattoo.

11. Granite block walls refers to time spent in the Old Folsom Prison.

12. Cell window with sun or bird = Waiting to be released.

13. Female crying face = has a loved one waiting for him to emerge.

14. SUR = Southerner.

15. Norteano refers to Northerner.

16. Prison block wall with falling bricks = on the inside, wishing to escape.

Monsters and Demons

As tattoos, depictions of devils and monsters on the flesh have the same psychological and spiritual effect as representations of skulls and bones.

The monster's symbolic aim is to shield the wearer from bad spirits who may mistake the beast for a part of or protector of the wearer.

The most frequently used monster motif is that of devils, gargoyles, winged monsters, and dragons. Many of these tattoos are created specifically for the purpose of creating anthropomorphic creatures.

Symbols of the East

Thousands of Eastern religious symbols originate in countries such as China, Japan, Tibet, and Thailand.

Perhaps the most well-known of these symbols is the lotus flower, which represents the unity of all beings with universal consciousness. The emblem represents the six syllables of Tibetan Buddhism's holy mantra ("OM Mani Padme Hum"), which together make a very potent symbol of balance, emancipation, and enlightenment.

Another common symbol is the OM, which is made up of several curlicues. The emblem is the most venerable Hindu symbol of spiritual understanding, the greatest name of God. Numerous traditions employ the sign for meditation and its associated syllables as a potent mantra.

The Yin-Yang sign is a dynamic representation of the flow and interplay of the two polar forces of male and female that surround creation in their entirety.

Enso, which translates as 'circle' in Japanese, is a single brushstroke painting. It is a Zen icon representing the true nature of existence and enlightenment.

Chinese Symbols are attractive for contemplative, ornamental, and talismanic use today due to their beauty and antiquity. Chinese symbols such as the "Double Happiness Sign" and the characters that make up each of the Chinese astrological signs are included.

Egyptian

Egyptian tattoos are frequently used to indicate a passion for the occult. The eye of Horus is the most popular tattoo design, as it is a strong emblem of protection, health, and wisdom. Egyptian tattoo themes including goddesses such as Isis, the Goddess of Wisdom, and Bastet, a goddess with a cat's head, are very popular.

Pixies, Nymphs, and Fairies

These mythical creatures, who have existed in every culture since before the birth of Christ, are particularly popular for women's tattoos. The majority of designs are derived from Celtic or British art.

Fantasy

Dragons, magicians, and unicorns are the most popular fantasy figures.

Wizards are connected with pagan and Celtic magic due to their long cloaks and white beards. Images from the Lord of the Rings and Harry Potter have been incorporated into modern renditions.

The dragon is a significant protective symbol in Celtic, Greek, Roman, Japanese, and Chinese cultures. They also symbolize a propensity for the occult and mystical powers.

Unicorns symbolize the individual's uniqueness and fragility, and are a popular tattoo image among young females.

Flames

Fires are a prevalent motif in tattooing, whether they represent the purifying quality of holy fire or the searing flames of Hell. One reason for this could be because flames create a vivid backdrop for a tattoo, allowing it to truly stand out.

Motorcycles in flames, newborns in flames, sacred hearts in flames, crucifixes in flames, and skulls in flames are all popular motifs.

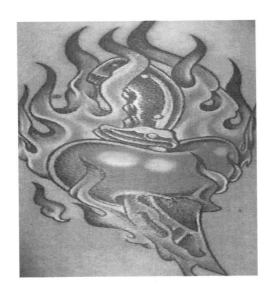

Fauna and Flora

Flowers are a very prevalent motif in tattoo art, whether they are enormous and complex, little and modest, or part of the background of a tattoo. The rose, with its associations with romance and fidelity, is undoubtedly the most popular flower.

The following is a list of popular flowers and their associated symbolic meanings:

- ✓ Amaryllis - pride, pastoral poetry
- ✓ Anemone – abandoned
- ✓ Aster - love, daintiness
- ✓ Azalea - take care of yourself for me, temperance, fragile desire, Chinese emblem of womanhood
- ✓ Bluebell – humility

- ✓ Cactus – fortitude
- ✓ Camellia (pink) - yearning for you
- ✓ Camellia (red) - you're a blaze in my heart
- ✓ Camellia (white) - you're adorable
- ✓ Carnation (striped) - I wish I could be with you
- ✓ Carnation (red) - adoration, my heart aches for you
- ✓ Carnation (white) - delicate and lovely, innocence, pure love, a woman's good luck flower
- ✓ Cattail - tranquillity and prosperity
- ✓ Chrysanthemum (white) – truth

- ✓ Chrysanthemum (yellow) - betrayed love
- ✓ Crocus – joy
- ✓ Cyclamen - resignation and farewell
- ✓ Daffodil - regard, unrequited love, you're the only one, the sun always shines when I'm with you
- ✓ Daisy - innocence, devoted love, I'll never tell, purity
- ✓ Dandelion - faithfulness, happiness
- ✓ Fern - enchantment, allure, assurance, and refuge
- ✓ Fir – time
- ✓ Forget-me-not - true love, memories

- ✓ Gardenia - you're wonderful, secret love
- ✓ Heather (lavender) - appreciation, loneliness
- ✓ Heather (white) - protection, manifests wishes
- ✓ Holly - domestic tranquillity
- ✓ Hyacinth (blue) – steadfastness
- ✓ Hyacinth (white) - beauty, I'll pray for you
- ✓ Iris - fleur-de-lis, France's national flower, your friendship means so much to me, faith, hope, knowledge, and heroism, my compliments
- ✓ Ivy - wedded love, fidelity, friendship, and affection

- ✓ Jonquil - love me, reciprocate my affection, desire, sympathy, and the want for returned affection
- ✓ Lily (white) - virginity, purity, grandeur, it's heavenly to be with you
- ✓ Lily (yellow) - I'm cheerful and I'm walking on air.
- ✓ Lily (calla) - beauty, remembrance
- ✓ Lily (day) - coquetry, Chinese mother's emblem
- ✓ Lily (tiger) - wealth, pride
- ✓ Lily of the valley - humility, virgin Mary's tears, return to happiness, sweetness, you've made my life complete

- ✓ Magnolia – nobility
- ✓ Mistletoe - kiss me, affection, to overcome difficulties, sacred Indian plant
- ✓ Myrtle - love, Hebrew symbol of marriage
- ✓ Narcissus - remain as sweet as you are
- ✓ Orange flower - innocence, eternal love, marriage, and fruitfulness
- ✓ Orchid - Chinese symbol for many children, refinement, beauty, love, beautiful lady,
- ✓ Palm leaves - victorious and prosperous
- ✓ Peony - prosperous life, prosperous marriage

- ✓ Poppy (generic) - endless slumber, oblivion, fantasy
- ✓ Poppy (red) – pleasure
- ✓ Poppy (white) – consolation
- ✓ Poppy (yellow) - prosperity and success
- ✓ Primrose - I can't live without you
- ✓ Rose (bridal) - joyful love
- ✓ Rose (dark crimson) – lamentation
- ✓ Rose (hibiscus) - delectable fragrance
- ✓ Rose (leaf) - you may hope
- ✓ Rose (pink) - ideal happiness, please believe me
- ✓ Rose (red) - I love you
- ✓ Rose (tea) - I'll never forget

- ✓ Rose (thornless) - instantaneous love
- ✓ Rose (white) - innocence and purity, I am worthy of you, you are divine, secrecy and silence
- ✓ Rose (white and red combined) - union, flower emblem of England
- ✓ Rose (white-dried) - death is preferable to loss of virtue
- ✓ Rosebud - youth and beauty, an innocent heart of love
- ✓ Rosebud (red) - pure and lovely
- ✓ Rosebud (white) – girlhood

- ✓ Roses (bouquet of mature blooms) – gratitude
- ✓ Roses (single full bloom) – I'll continue to love you, I love you
- ✓ Snapdragon - gracious lady
- ✓ Spider flower - elope with me
- ✓ Tulip (generic) - ideal lover, frame, Holland's flower emblem
- ✓ Tulip (red) - believe me, declaration of love
- ✓ Tulip (variegated) - eye-catching
- ✓ Tulip (yellow) - your grin radiates sunshine

- ✓ Violet (blue) - vigilance, faithfulness, I will always be true
- ✓ Violet (white) - dare to dream
- ✓ Zinnia (mixed) - contemplation (or recollection) of an absent friend
- ✓ Zinnia (scarlet) – constancy
- ✓ Zinnia (white) – goodness
- ✓ Zinnia (yellow) - a constant reminder
- ✓ Zinnia (magenta) - everlasting love

Goth

The preoccupation with existentialism, despair, and anarchy is what defines the Goth culture. Tattoos are typically dark, Nordic, or Germanic in style and reflect an interest in medieval, Victorian, and Edwardian history.

The Christian cross, the Egyptian ankh (a sign of eternal life), the

Egyptian "eye of Horus", the German Iron Cross, and the Satanic inverted pentacle are all common Goth symbols. Goth culture is also associated with bats, griffins, and depictions of the "undead" and howling spirits.

Griffins

Originally adornments for ancient architecture's turrets, these mythical winged animals are today the spiritual protectors of the human body. Griffins are particularly popular among bikers, Goths, Wiccans, and pagan communities.

Hearts and Symbols of Love

The Heart emblem is self-explanatory, having long served as the global symbol for love between the sexes.

Logos

Logos can be wise sayings, such as the legendary Hell's Angels motto "Born for Fun, Loyal to None," or they might truly mean anything corporate. Indeed, the latest craze among corporate types is to get their company's emblem tattooed somewhere. This is particularly true for Apple's computer company, which today boasts something dubbed "The Apple Tattoo Cult."

Almost any logo or catchphrase can be transformed into a tattoo. Indeed, logo perversions are extremely popular in tattoos. The image of the cocaine spoon with Coca-Cola beneath it and the slogan "It's The Real Thing" is an illustration of this.

Mermaids

Mermaids have a variety of meanings for various individuals. They symbolize sailors' rescue from drowning at sea. Mermaids symbolize female sexuality and a dependence on intuition for women.

Life in the Ocean and Rivers

Fish, whales, crabs, and dolphins are the most often tattooed sea creatures.

Fish have been associated with messiahs and saviors throughout history. The ithycus fish, a Christian emblem, is made up of two basic curved and crossed lines and denotes renewing faith.

Carp symbolize love and bravery in China. Goldfish serve as an evocative representation of gold money. Salmon are also associated with love and courage in North American Native Indian legends, owing to their ability to swim upstream to spawning sites. Pisces, the Western zodiac sign, is also connected with fish.

Crabs are also a popular topic for tattoos, owing to their association with the Cancerian zodiac sign.

Whale tattoos are frequently used to advocate for the creature's ecological problems. Whales are associated with overcoming despair and "the dark night of the soul" in the majority of cultures, as well as with aligning oneself with the element of water.

In Western culture, dolphins symbolize joy and peace. The animal is believed to bring departed spirits to their future incarnation in South Pacific and Native American traditions.

Good and Evil Pin-Up Girls

The saying "a sailor has a lady in every port" refers to pin up girl tattoos. South Pacific explorers returned home with tattoos of their exotic female discoveries on their arms. Certain tattoo designs were transformed into goddess-like creatures believed to protect men at sea.

During World Wars I and II, the pin up tattoo became popular, coinciding with the rise of magazine pin up heroines. Armed men's forearms were emblazoned with images of the Gibson girl and Betty Grable. Marilyn Monroe and Rita Hayworth photographs were very famous during the Korean War.

The lighter pin-up female tattoos were inspired by famous women. The evil side of this concept was symbolized by goddesses, witches, Viking Queens,

Amazons, and anthropomorphic monsters.

Portraits Realism

Simply as a statement of affection for one's family, it is a common custom in the South Americas to get one's children and wife tattooed somewhere on the body so that they can accompany you everywhere you go. Typically, these are photorealistic portraits rendered in fine-line and black and grey.

Religious – Symbols of Faith and Spirituality

Religious symbols include crosses, prayer hands, flaming holy vessels, and doves.

Additionally, complete replicas of the Crucifixion and other well-known biblical scenes are extremely prevalent. Devout adherents frequently have fully landscaped mythology tattooed on their backs, chests, and arms, including scenes from The Last Supper and to-scale copies of iconic works such as the Sistine Chapel.

Tribal

Tribal tattoos are typically black and white with strong organic motifs such as horns and branches. Numerous cultures have influenced the tribal style, including Native American, Maori,

African, Celtic, and Viking traditions.

Tattoo Motifs for Wiccans and Pagans

Everything Celtic, angelic, flamboyant, bony, demonic, druidic, natural, or heavenly can be incorporated into a Wiccan or pagan tattoo. The huge assortment of symbols that reflect the several sects associated with these religions includes images of Gods or Goddesses or their emblems.

The Rose Cross is a central emblem in the Western Mystery Tradition, dating all the way back to the Rosicrucians. It is a holistic sign that combines aspects of Kabbalah, alchemy, astrology, and esoteric Christianity, and so on.

Horus's Eye is an ancient Egyptian protective, health, and wisdom sign. It originated in the mythological conflict between Horus and Set over Set's assassination of Horus' father, the deity Osiris.

The lemniscate, a sign representing infinity, eternity, the numinous, and higher spiritual energies, is sometimes referred to as an 'eight on its side.'

The Triquetra is a lovely trinitarian emblem found

frequently in Gothic and Celtic art. Although it is frequently used in Pagan or Christian contexts, it can be used to denote a wide variety of three-fold systems.

Spirals are a frequent natural shape and an ancient mystical symbol. It embodies the energies and patterns that govern both creation and evolution, as well as self-transformation.

CHAPTER FIVE

WHERE TO FIND DESIGNS

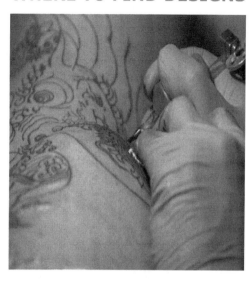

Heart-Centered   Design Inspiration

Any tattoo artist will tell you that the best place to look for inspiration is within your heart. However, the design you have in your heart may not be the most practical for you. Additionally, it may be tough to convey your emotions to the tattoo artist, who is, after all, sitting there with a tattoo needle poised to brand you for life. It is strongly recommended that you bring a template or design with you when you see the tattoo artist, as a tattoo, like a diamond, is permanent.

Artistic Inspiration

The finest locations to get tattoo design ideas that you may take to the tattoo parlor are the library or everyone's favorite all-in-one resource - the Internet. Indeed, avoid going to the library entirely. This is only necessary if you do not have access to a computer or wish to have a full reproduction of Delacroix's work tattooed in fine detail on your back.

However, before you begin your Internet search, you should determine which period of art most appeals to you. Which artist appeals to you more: Andy Warhol or Leonardo Da Vinci? Do you like the swirls of color associated with Chinese art or the woodblock etching effect associated with Japanese and Medieval style tattoos? Which style do you prefer, realism or caricature? Or are they anagrams of company logos? All of these are critical questions to ask yourself prior to entering those all-important keywords into search engines.

The following artistic keywords should be entered into your search engine to locate examples of art that will inspire your tattoo: "astrological symbols," "expressionism," "flowers," "fantasy art," "gods," "goddesses," "goth art," "native American," "neo-primitivism," and "modernism." Others are "photorealism," "planetary symbols," "primitivism," "romantism," and "surrealism," "symbols," and "religious symbols," "indigenous art," "woodblock," "tattoos," and "tattoo symbols."

Using the Internet to Design Your Tattoo

By entering the phrase "tattoo" into your search engine, you'll be sent to a plethora of websites offering what are known as flash or stock tattoos, which you can occasionally obtain for free or for a little cost. These are the same types of graphics that are frequently shown on tattoo parlor walls. The concept is that you may take these templates to a tattoo artist and have the image replicated on your body.

Typically, the tattoo artist may also somewhat customize the tattoo for you, either by adding stripes, rays, or bars, initials, vines and flowers, flames, or other "fill work" that contributes to the tattoo's uniqueness.

www.findatattoo.com is one of the most incredible online sites for stock and flash tattoos, with over 6,000 online flash and stock tattoos stored in its virtual gallery.

Additionally, there are computer applications available to assist you in designing your own tattoo. Symnet is one of the greatest, since it enables you to make your own tribal bespoke designs with pinpoint accuracy in a matter of seconds. This program, which is excellent for generating personalized arm bands and anklet designs, may be accessed at http://www.symynet.com/tattoo_designs/tattoo-designs-home.htm.

http://www.createatattoo.com is another amazing resource that will truly get your creative juices flowing. This little-known website enables you to make your own bespoke tribal tattoo in just two minutes, even if you have no creative ability whatsoever.

Simply select a design, modify it, and print it out to bring to the tattoo artist.

If your design incorporates letters, you might enjoy perusing the hundreds of odd typefaces available at http://www.fontmagic.com.
These fonts enable you to download a variety of unique styles, including Roman and Gothic lettering, which are notoriously difficult to come across for free.

CHAPTER SIX

CHOOSING A TATTOO ARTIST

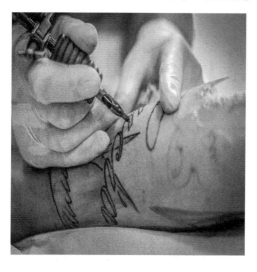

Reputation is Critical

Tattoo artists are classified into two groups: those who have received official instruction or have completed an apprenticeship and "scratchers.'

The scratcher is a self-taught tattoo artist who, while artistically brilliant, rarely sterilizes his implements. While the scratcher may work from a studio, he frequently does it from his house, cellar, or back area of a pub. They may self-identify as freelancers. A scratcher frequently acquires equipment over the Internet or email. The worst aspect of a scratcher is their proclivity for reusing needles, which can result in lethal infections such as hepatitis or AIDS.

The artists who lack artistic ability fall halfway between the sloppy practices of the scratcher and the highly lit, sterile studios of professional tattoo artists. Their tattoos are poorly produced, with uneven outlines, unappealing colors, and an out-of-proportion sketching perspective. If the works of a tattoo artist if anything is ill-conceived or lacks a pleasing composition, heed your instincts and keep away.

Unfortunately, we live in a period when tattooing can literally kill a consumer if correct protocols are not followed. Needles and equipment must be sterilized properly, and stringent cross-contamination and sterilization protocols must be followed, or disease might spread rapidly. Blood-borne viruses do cause death among tattoo clients. If you believe that all you need to acquire a tattoo is a needle and some ink, you are mistaken!

Before you choose a tattoo artist, you must make an internal commitment that you will not accept mundane, uninteresting, or sloppy work. There is much too much skill on the market for you to end up with a tattoo that is poorly sketched or splotchy in appearance.

It is ultimately your job to select an artist who possesses the sterility of a surgeon and the drawing ability of a master. This may entail paying some money or traveling to another location to have the tattoo you desire. You must convince yourself that this investment of time and energy is worthwhile, as it results in a permanent work of art.

The only way to judge a tattoo artist correctly is to view examples of his or her work. They should have a portfolio that is in some way signed or watermarked. The portfolio should include images of their previous work. Additionally, you can visit the shop or studio and request to observe the artist in action. One compelling reason to do so is to ascertain the artist's portfolio's veracity. Regrettably, anyone can display tattoo examples on their walls and claim originality of the work.

Another technique to discover a good tattoo artist is to approach someone who has a tattoo you admire and inquire about the artist. If the tattooist is good, they will be the first to suggest him or her. Ensure that you question these persons about the expense of the tattoo as well as the shop's sanitary facilities. Strangers are more likely to give you better advice than your friends in this scenario. The issue with a friend is that they may be a "friend of a friend" of the tattooist but may have no knowledge of the tattooist's artistic or business reputation.

Magazines devoted to industry and culture are also excellent sources of knowledge on tattoos. The purpose of the majority of these periodicals is to separate the scratchers from the great artists and to highlight the best in tattooing.

Expect the Moon and the Stars but Not the Moon and the Stars

As with other artists, tattoo artists have their own distinct styles in which they shine and styles in which they fall short. For instance, if you want a realistic depiction of Marilyn Monroe tattooed on your arm, avoid an artist who specializes in replicating gruesome cartoons.

When it comes to tattooing, you are ultimately the art director, choosing the talent to bring your vision to life. Certain tattoo artists excel at fine line work, while others excel at the rhythms and motifs associated with primitive work. Still others excel at flowers rather than flaming skulls. Generally, you can know by inspecting the artist's in-shop picture collection, regardless of whether they excel at vibrant classical work or the subtle shading required to achieve photorealism.

The majority of tattoo artists are passionate about their work and are willing to "get into the spirit" with you in order to determine the type and size of tattoo that is perfect for you. If the artist makes size and color suggestions, heed the artist's advice. They may simply know what looks best, or they may be attempting to quietly communicate something about their own talent limitations.

Once seated, show your tattoo artist respect. Make no attempt to be a "back seat" artist and bother the artist with rash creative proposals. Of course, this will not occur if you and the artist have previously agreed on an appropriate design.

Cost is a Consideration

If you are unable to afford a tattoo, then accept your situation. While a tattoo is irreplaceable, it can also be viewed as a type of "beauty treatment." You would not allow a terrible hairdresser to ruin your hair, so do not allow an affordable tattoo artist to permanently brand you with a design you despise.

As is the case with every commodity, the price of a tattoo varies according to the artist. Ones who are well-known or have won awards will always charge more than inexperienced artists.

A flash or stock tattoo is the least expensive type of tattoo. These are the designs found on the studio, parlor, and (traditionally) barber shop walls. While artists typically charge a flat rate for their flash creations, this is subject to the size of the design and the amount of color used to saturate it. In general, anticipate to pay between $50 and $100 in the United States for a tattoo measuring approximately two by two square inches.

Most artists charge by the hour for custom work. It is strongly advised that you bring your template or design with you so that the artist can provide you with an exact estimate of the time required to complete the task. Custom tattoos cost between $50 and $300 per hour in the United States. Although price does not always equate to artist brilliance, you are likely to acquire a tattoo that you are satisfied with if you choose an artist that charges $150 per hour or more.

Considerations for Professionals

Applying a tattoo entails much more than simply creating a pleasing image. A professional artist is a combination of an artist and a technician, as well as a craftsperson. Selecting the artist who will apply your tattoo is the most critical decision you will make, therefore ensure that the artist is a mix of doctor and artist.

Ascertain that you devote sufficient time to scrutinizing the artist's work. Do the tattoos' lines appear wobbly or feathery? Do the circles and squares appear to be circles and squares, respectively? How about the color scheme? Are the colors blended evenly to produce a sense of dimension, depth, and shading? Are there any tattoos that appear bloated, fading, blurry, or out of proportion? When it comes to this, trust your creative instincts, as despite any assurances or justifications for subpar work, your tattoo will almost certainly match what is in the artist's portfolio in the end.

Tattooing is a sort of invasive surgery since it requires bonding color to the skin's basal layer. Once the tattoo has healed, the more translucent outer layer of the skin develops over it.

When a tattoo "fails," it is typically due to the ink being injected too deeply into the skin, where physiological fluids can cause the tattoo to spread and lose definition. If the tattoo is not pressed deeply enough into the skin, it will fade or remove entirely.

Additionally, you may like to ascertain whether the artist complies with city or state rules and what certifications and licenses are required to tattoo legally in your city or state. If the artist is unable to produce this certification, do not take a chance.

Evaluating an Artist's Practice

If the tattoo studio does not appear to be as clean as your doctor's or dentist's office, exit immediately. The following settings are not appropriate for tattooing: someone's kitchen, a neighborhood pub, the bleachers at a racetrack, or during a county fair. This is because certain surroundings do not allow for the maintenance of sterile conditions.

Observing the artist perform is also recommended, as all equipment used to apply the tattoo should be sanitized or disposable. For example, the artist's needle should not be dipped into a huge plastic container of ink. The ink should be poured into a single-use container.

Additionally, you may choose to examine how the tattooist applies ointments and Vaseline. To apply these ingredients to your skin, the tattoo artist should always use a steel or disposable wooden sterilized spreader, never a finger.

Additionally, the tattooist should wear disposable sterile latex gloves. If he or she is touching you with bare fingers, you are at risk of infection and sickness. Additionally, each tattoo should be performed with a new sterilized needle.

All non-disposable equipment should be autoclave sterilized after each use. Equipment is not sterilized with ultrasonic cleaning. It should be used solely to clean the equipment prior to placing it in the autoclave. Ascertain that the artist possesses an FDA-regulated autoclave by questioning him or her. Sterilizing tattooing equipment by immersing it in a tub of rubbing alcohol is insufficient.

Before starting the tattoo, many artists may apply roll-on deodorant to make a darker impression of the transfer copy on your skin. Although this method of transferring a stock tattoo to the skin is quite effective, take in mind that the deodorant may have been used on the skin of another client. The deodorant should be wiped onto a tissue, and then the tissue should be used to apply it to your skin.

Additionally, you may wish to inquire about the artist's Hepatitis B vaccination status. Never accept someone's word for it. Do they have evidence? Can they produce a doctor's document attesting to their vaccination? Hepatitis vaccine is a three-shot series administered over a four-month period. This is not something that will slip someone's memory. Getting a hepatitis vaccine is "a once-in-a-lifetime experience."

Regrettably, mandated hepatitis B testing is not necessary prior to an artist picking up a needle. To ensure your maximum safety, get vaccinated before to get a new tattoo.

Signs You've Arrived to the Correct Studio

1. **The Tattoo Artist Provides Previous Work Samples**

Never choose an artist who is unable to present a portfolio. A photo album of tattoos done on living flesh should be available in the studio for you to peruse. A well-executed display of stock tattoos on the walls does not suffice to establish the artist's reputation.

2.   **The Tattoo Artist Is a Disposable Character in a Disposable Universe**

Nothing used by the tattoo artist should ever be returned to its container. This category encompasses ointment, ink, and water. These compounds have often come into touch with your blood plasma. Such frugality raises the chance of infection spreading to you and others.

Always store ink in ink caps, which are small cups that hold just enough color to tattoo you. Never return this ink to a bottle or jar.

3. The Tattoo Artist Is Certified to Use an Autoclave

An autoclave is a type of electric sterilizer that resembles a pressure cooker made of steel. Physicians use it to sanitize medical equipment. To sterilize equipment, it must sit in the autoclave for at least thirty minutes at a temperature of 246 degrees.

Possessing an autoclave does not imply that it is in use. Inquire whether the artist has a current autoclave certificate indicating that the unit is frequently checked and in use by the business's operators.

If the tattoo artist exhibits any "attitude" toward you, is evasive about the usage of the autoclave, or attempts to pass off an ultrasonic cleaner as sterilization equipment, exit immediately.

4. **The Tattoo Artist Makes Use of New, Sanitized Needles**

Each time, new sterile needles are extracted from an autoclave bag. Needles should not be removed from this bag until the tattooing process is complete. Each autoclave needle bag is often labelled with a little label referred to as a "sterile confirmation" label along with the manufacturer's name. If you do not see this label on your bag or if your needles are not inside, the artist may be recycling materials.

The new needles are a brilliant silver tone. If the needles appear discolored, brownish, or dulled, the treatment should be halted.

5. The Tattoo Artist is protected by Latex Gloves

Fingers are the most effective way to transfer germs to raw, freshly tattooed flesh. As such, the tattoo artist must always wear standard medical latex gloves. Gloves should be free of holes and tears and fit the artist adequately. A pinhole in a latex glove is all it takes to raise the danger of cross contamination.

6. The Tattoo Artist Properly Disposes of Needles Using a Sharps Container

Sharps containers are typically red plastic containers with a biohazard emblem on the outside. Additionally, you will notice these bins labelled "hazardous waste" in dentist and physician offices.

Used needles and other contaminated items that are not scheduled for autoclave sterilization should be placed in these containers and promptly removed.

7. **The Artist Possess a Permit to Practice**

Most states require tattoo artists to obtain a license before they can use a needle on anyone. Consult your state's laws to ensure you are working with a licensed practitioner.

8. **The Artist Has Undergone Training and Certification**

Regrettably, no official accreditation is granted to tattoo artists who complete their course.

Tattooing is an oral tradition that is typically passed down through apprenticeships. However, the majority of tattoo artists will be capable to demonstrate that they have been trained in safe and hygienic tattooing methods by a reputable tattoo artist.

9. **The Tattoo Studio is a Clean and Well-Lit Environment**

While the majority of tattoo shops have a Goth aesthetic, complete with dark lights and loud stereo music, this does not indicate the establishment is filthy. What is critical is that the "surgical" space be clean and well-lit with halogen lights.

10. **"Click" with your Tattoo Artist**

You must show reverence and regard for the tattoo artist, and he or she must show you the same reverence and respect. You are not required to become best friends, but this is not the time for ridicule, sarcasm, or demonstrations of creative temperament. Among the behaviors that come under the category of artistic temperament are rage, giddiness, an unwillingness to adhere to a schedule, and an invitation to get high or intoxicated. Additionally, a tattoo artist should not believe himself or herself to be too cool to handle oneself in the respectful and courteous manner associated with sound business procedures.

CHAPTER SEVEN

GETTING INKED

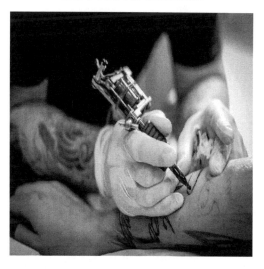

Where to Put It?

Pain is frequently a decisive factor in picking where to place a tattoo, however certainly some folks will want to place their tattoo where it is least or most disguised by clothing or where they believe is spiritually fitting. For example, a long-distance runner may choose to tattoo of the winged god Mercury on his or her ankle to increase speed, but an adulterous woman may choose to tattoo her lover's name between her two front toes so that her husband will never see it.

The Factor of Pain

Where is it most painful to get a tattoo? Although most would answer the wallet, the most painful regions are believed to be the stomach, spine, and chest in males and in women, the ankle, spine, and ribcage.

The buttocks, arm, and back are believed to be the least

uncomfortable places for men. The stomach, buttocks, thigh, and shoulder are the least uncomfortable places for women.

What You Can Expect

After you've chosen a design and discussed the technique with the tattooist, you'll be scheduled for an appointment.

It is critical to abstain from aspirin-based pain drugs before the surgery, as these medications thin the blood. Aspirin-based drugs may exacerbate bleeding and impair your body's natural capacity to heal.

When you arrive at the tattoo shop, the tattoo artist will often offer you a stencil generated from your design. Certain tattoo artists use special thermal paper to produce a rapid transfer. This is your final opportunity to reverse your decision.

The majority of tattoo establishments require payment in advance. This is to ensure that they get compensated regardless of whether you approve of the ultimate result. Satisfaction is not guaranteed in the tattooing business. Refunds are as challenging to acquire.

Prior to tattooing, the majority of tattooists would require proof of age and contact information in case of an emergency. This is mandatory in some countries, such as Canada. In several Asian countries, the tattooist has the choice to reject you as a subject.

The Chair

After the exchange of money and the completion of the necessary paperwork, you will be seated in some type of tattoo chair. This is typically done in a private space, such as a booth or a separate room. While many tattooists work from a dentist's chair or an Easy Boy rocker, some may work from an ordinary chair. Additionally, you may be asked if you mind if another prospective client observes the process.

Canvas Preparation

Once seated in the chair, the area to be tattooed is cleaned with a cleaning solution (usually rubbing alcohol). If the area is hairy, the tattooist will shave an area somewhat larger than the design's size. Assure that the tattooist uses a new, disposable razor to shave you.

The tattoo artist will then confirm the transfer's precise placement on your skin. Occasionally, the skin is moistened with a scream or a swab of roll-on deodorant, which enhances the visibility of the transfer from the skin. Following that, the reverse-image transfer is pressed and placed to the skin for a few minutes.

After removing the paper, you should notice a bluish outline of your artwork. The majority of tattooists will ask you to inspect the tattoo location in the mirror. If you dislike the appearance of the tattoo, this is your final opportunity to pull out of the situation.

After donning plastic latex gloves, the tattooist will take some time pouring pigments from large jugs into small disposable cups called ink caps. He or she will next retrieve sterilized needles from an autoclave bag and prepare additional supplies for the surgery, such as Vaseline and ointments.

Outline Creation

A little layer of ointment will be applied to the region to be tattooed. This ointment cleanses the skin, secures the transfer, and enables the needle to glide more easily across the skin.

As is the case with dentist drills, the sound of a tattoo machine is significantly worse than the discomfort. If you are seriously concerned by buzzing sounds, it is recommended that you put on stereo headphones and listen to music to drown out the noise and relax.

The tattoo artist will load the tattooing machine with the required needles. Typically, the artist will use a thicker needle to trace the transfer's outline in black. Depending on the size and complexity of the design, the tattoo machine will regularly stop and clean your skin with a cotton swab to remove any oozing blood.

The majority of people report that the most painful element of obtaining a tattoo is establishing the design's black outline.

Although it can be somewhat painful, the discomfort normally subsides quickly afterwards.

After completing the outline, the tattoo artist will wash away any lingering bluish marks created by the transfer technique.

Color Application

After the tattoo artist completes the outline, he or she will add shading and color. You're likely to get a moment to catch your breath as the tattooist switches the needles on the machine.

While color inking might be unpleasant, it is a distinct experience from black outlining. Most people find it less unpleasant than sitting through the process of generating the tattoo's black and white outline.

The duration of the process is determined by the size of the design and the number of colors required to achieve the desired appearance. Extremely huge designs may require multiple trips to complete.

CHAPTER EIGHT

TAKING CARE OF YOUR TATTOO

Post-Operative Care

Post-Operative Care is a term that refers to the period following surgery.

You are responsible for the post-operative care of your tattoo the moment you walk out the front door of the tattoo shop. The way you take care of your tattoo in the coming days and weeks will decide how sharp and clear it is for the rest of your life.

Do not remove the bandage in an attempt to "air out" your tattoo. Keep the bandage on for as long as your tattoo artist suggests. Some tattooists would advise you to leave the bandage on for up to twenty-four hours, while others will advise you to wait at least three to six hours before looking at your artwork.

When it's time to take the bandage off, go slowly and carefully. Remember to always wash your hands before touching your tattoo or the area around it. If the bandage is stuck to your skin, don't pull on it or try to yank it off. Wet the bandage with warm water until the moisture loosens it, then peel it away carefully.

When the tattoo is exposed, properly clean the area with warm soapy water. Using a soft, clean towel, pat (not rub) the area dry. Try to avoid wetting the tattoo in the bath or shower for the first week.

Some tattooists advise leaving the tattoo exposed to the air for 10 minutes after removing the bandage, while others advise treating the area with ointment right away. The tattooist will usually advise you to apply an antibacterial cream like Bactine or a specific tattoo cream like Tattoo Goo on the inked area. If you experience an allergic reaction to any ointment, make sure to tell your tattoo artist right away. If the response is severe, he or she will propose an alternative or advise you to seek medical help.

The Recovery Process

Remember to clean and reapply ointment to your new tattoo at least twice a day for the amount of days your tattoo artist has recommended. Typically, you'll be instructed to apply the ointment for three days. Some tattooists will advise you to do so till the tattoo has scabbed, while others will advise you to do so until it has healed.

Continue to keep the region clean and use a lotion after washing with warm soapy water to keep the tattooed skin supple after you stop using the ointment.

The new tattoo will begin to peel and scab at the three-day mark. If your tattoo has a lot of scabbing, it's likely that it was badly inked.

As the tattoo heals, it is typical for it to appear blurry or cloudy for a few days. This is called "Onion Skin," and it is a natural component of the healing process. If your tattoo only appears clear while moist, you're dealing with Onion Skin.

The most important aspect of post-operative tattoo care is to keep the tattoo clean and moisturized. After the wound has healed, apply the ointment and then a lotion to help the skin regain its pliability and suppleness. Make no attempt to hasten the process in any manner. Allow your body's amazing natural healing mechanisms to take their course, and everything will be fine.

Shaving a Tattoo

If you have a tattoo on an area of your body where you would regularly shave, such as your face or legs, you must wait for the tattoo to fully heal before shaving again. You can shave around the tattoo, but make sure that no shaving foam, cream, or hair gets into the tattoo.

You must not shave the tattoo until the skin above it has completely healed. Wait a little longer if there is any scabbing or peeling. It's safe to resume shaving when you can't distinguish the difference between the surrounding region and the flesh around the tattoo. If the skin around the tattoo appears rosy or angry, don't use a razor on it.

After you've re-shaved the area, make sure to moisturize it properly to keep the skin healthy.

Aftercare for Tattoos: The Golden Rules

1. Don't scratch the tattoo if it itch. Scabs should not be picked, rubbed, or pressed against your body. You can try gently patting the region with the flat side of (your very clean) fingertips to relieve the itching. During the initial few days of healing, it is entirely

possible to scratch the ink straight out of the tattoo!

2. Stay out of the light as much as possible. The tattoo may become discolored as a result of this. A sunburn on top of a tattoo can be extremely painful. Applying sunscreen on a tattoo is not a good idea. Instead, opt for long sleeves. You can apply sunscreen to your tattoo when it has completely healed to protect it and prevent it from fading.

3. Stay away from salty water. The sun and the sea are

tattoos' deadliest enemies. A fresh wound can hurt and become sensitive to infections and fading if exposed to salt water.

Tattoo Touch-up

A tattoo may need to be re-inked from time to time for many reasons. Return to the tattooist for an educated judgment if you believe your tattoo requires additional work. Unless you have visibly picked and ripped the tattoo completely off your body, most tattoo artists are prepared to repair fading or unset work for free.

After you've had your tattoo re-inked, you'll need to follow the same post-operative care guidelines as you did before: keep it clean, moisturized, avoid soaking it, and stay out of the sun and surf.

I Despise My Tattoo

If you don't like your tattoo, talk to the artist about getting a cover-up. Tattoo artists frequently use stock designs to cover up offending tattoos. Large blocks of black and images such as black panthers, black clouds, and other chunky designs are common in these designs.

Without resorting to blotting out your tattoo with a massive black mass, a skilled tattoo artist can replace it. For a cover-up work, though, you'll need a talented artist. You'll need a custom design that completely replaces the current one. Cover-up work is difficult and time-consuming, so expect to spend more for a cover-up piece than for a new tattoo. Choose an artist who has a good sense of design.

Reworking a tattoo is another way to make the damaged body area more appealing. It's not uncommon for a tattoo to require some form of enhancement. If your tattoo is faded, jagged, or uneven, you should consider reworking it. Any good tattooist will also correct any color skips or outlining issues that may arise after the item has healed. Bars, borders, rainbows, and flora and fauna can all be used to beautify tattoos.

CHAPTER NINE

REMOVAL OF TATOO

It's Too Late for You

You've spent hours picking out your design, enduring the discomfort in the chair, avoiding picking at the scab, and now you've decided you can't tolerate the look of the unsightly thing. You'd not be alone in this situation. Over half of those who get tattoos regret their decision.

This is likely due to the impulsive aspect addressed in chapter one, which warns against getting a tattoo when drunk, high, in love, or on vacation. This is why it is so essential to "think before you ink."

The majority of dermatologists will tell you that there is no way to completely remove tattoos. Although modern technology can effectively remove the majority of ink, they all leave some sort of imprint on your skin, whether it's a blemish, scar, or change in skin tone. It's difficult to say whether the cursed tattoo or the scarring left on the skin by removal methods is more terrible.

The ability to make your tattoo disappear is determined by several things, including your skin type, skin color, how well you recover, and the size of the tattoo. It also depends on the location of the tattoo on the body and the ink used, as there are many different types of ink used all over the world.

The majority of tattoo removal technology are effective at removing black ink, however color tattoos might be difficult to remove. In fact, after a tattoo removal therapy, some color tattoos experience even more discolouration and blotchiness!

Technology and Methods for Tattoo Removal

A tattoo can be removed in one of four methods. Because tattoo ink is designed to penetrate to the lowest layer of the epidermis, none of them are affordable or painless.

1. **Dermabrasion** - This method involves rubbing off the tattoo with an abrasive machine (such as a sander) or a chemical-based lotion.

2. **Excision** - This entails removing the tattoo

surgically and having the area stitched up by a doctor. In the case of little tattoos, this method works well. Large tattoos necessitate general anesthesia and a skin graft.

3. **Cyrosurgery** – The tattoo is surgically removed once the area of skin has been frozen. This works best with minor tattoos.

4. **Laser Surgery** - Lasers produce brief light pulses. This light penetrates the top layers of skin and into the pigment of the ink in the dermis when used for tattoo

removal. The pigment is broken down into smaller particles by the energy from the laser's light, which the body's immune system can then remove. Because the laser's wavelength is exclusively focused at the tattoo ink pigments, this procedure does not harm surrounding skin. This approach, however, is partially effectively on color tattoos because lasers operate best when there is a contrast of black ink against white skin. On persons who have darker complexion, laser removal does not function.

It is both costly and time consuming to remove tattoos. Tattoo removal can cost hundreds to thousands of dollars, and most health plans and insurance policies do not cover it.

Your doctor will most likely recommend you to a dermatologist, who may subsequently refer you to a dermatological surgeon. Alternatively, your tattooist might be able to refer you to a professional who specializes in tattoo removal. Make certain that the actual removal is done by a licensed medical practitioner, whatever you do.

Printed in Great Britain
by Amazon